Talgarth

in Photographs

Jewel of the Black Mountains

Volume 2

by Roger G. Williams

Foreword by
Richard Livsey

Old Bakehouse Publications

Abertillery

First published in December 1996

ISBN 1 874538 36 0

Published in the U.K. by
Old Bakehouse Publications
Church Street,
Abertillery, Gwent NP3 1EA
Telephone: 01495 212600   Fax: 01495 216222

Made and printed in the UK
by J.R. Davies (Printers) Ltd.

Foreword

Roger Williams has assembled an outstanding collection of old photographs of Talgarth and the surrounding district. His first book was an excellent mix, this one puts the icing on the cake!

I write this foreword as one who is a native of Talgarth, and who had the privilege of being brought up here. What memories this excellent book provoked for me, and I am sure many others. Cattle, sheep and horse sales too. The golden tongue of Howell Powell the auctioneer whose grasp of language was sufficient for me to describe accurately his style in my GCE O Level English Language essay. Thank you Howell, I passed the exam!

What I particularly remember is the kindness of so many local people. I had the misfortune to lose my father at the age of three, but everyone seemed to compensate for that and I survived through their good natured help. Talgarth was a democracy where everyone seemed to be equal.

Talgarth was a place, if I was absent, I just could not wait to get back to. My memory does not play tricks on me. The trains went literally everywhere and so punctual were they, you could tell the time of day. Catching trout in the Ennig. Scooping apple juice in cupped hands from the cider press outside the Castle or the New Inn. Watching unbroken ponies from the hills being caught in the street and being sold by a slap on the palms of buyer and seller. Sunday afternoon walks all the way to the top of the Black Mountains or Mynydd Troed, and back too. Bike rides to get aboard rowing boats on Llangorse Lake. Other cycle rides to the River Wye to jump across the rocks.

There were many traders, shops and businesses in Talgarth then. Both hospitals were fully occupied, and the staff at both (and more recent times) gave willingly of their expertise. The blacksmiths seemed to be able to make practically anything you requested. Shoeing horses was just routine.

This book clearly evokes happy memories through Roger's writing and these super photographs.

I believe, like in the town of Montgomery, a plaque should be put on the side of the Town Hall, listing the number of all the trades, businesses and farms in the Parish 50 years ago or 100 years ago. We would all get a shock. But I am certain it would encourage all to help rebuild the town of Talgarth and its district once again into a thriving and vibrant community. Our young people deserve it. They know, like I do and all who live or who have lived in Talgarth, it is set in a superb countryside location. All that is required is the will to make it happen for Talgarth again. There are hopeful signs now that this aim will indeed succeed.

Richard Livsey

Contents

Introduction

When Volume One of this book was published in August 1995, little did I realise the extent of approval and enthusiasm that a book on Talgarth would receive and for that, I am most grateful. An early reprint became necessary coupled with eager questions 'when will we see another one?' Fortunately I have received valued support from the good citizens of Talgarth and its neighbours who have loaned some of the photographs and information included in this second volume. This is typical of the close community spirit and attitudes which still prevail in our town. Another example of this was the success in 1996 of Talgarth's first Festival of the Black Mountains, an event which many hope will become an annual feature.

This Volume Two is another presentation of photographs and captions extending over a number of generations with the intent of reminding us of the many changes which have affected the area. The Mid-Wales Hospital for instance, which served so well its patients and the economy of Talgarth is but a short distance away from its demise. Similarly, the acclaimed Bronllys Hospital has diminished from its former self. Also included in these pages are a number of photographs of the inhabitants of the district who are involved in various activities and occupations and whose faces will be remembered by many readers. I sincerely hope that this second book will be as well received as its predecessor and that much pleasure will be gleaned from its pages.

Finally I would like to express my gratitude to fellow author and colleague Malcolm Thomas for his advice and encouragement in producing this second volume.

Roger G. Williams

CHAPTER 1

Talgarth Town

1. A peaceful setting at The Square in about 1954 and notably advertised at the Town Hall is a season of Dramatic Art productions. The Square was once a venue for markets and fairs and children would look forward to a visit from the man with the dancing bear. The bear danced and played the castinets while its owner collected money from onlookers. Man and bear were said to sleep under the hedges on the outskirts of the village.

Talgarth. Market Square.

2. When this picture was taken in 1903 local residents could do most of their shopping in Talgarth itself without travelling far, unlike today. On the hill can be seen a substantial retailer of general drapery, outfitting and dressmaking all under one roof.

3. The Tower Hotel which has been a commercial landmark of Talgarth for a century. This photograph is from the year 1904 and the external appearance has not changed too significantly. Closed for a while, this fine old hostelry has been refurbished and was re-opened in 1996 offering accommodation to the welcome tourist.

High Street, Talgarth

4. High Street Talgarth at one time housed quite a number of commercial premises as seen by this photograph of 1904. A three-storey hotel, a bookseller and stationer and the old Post Office are but a few examples of a thriving economy almost a century ago. Talgarth's first public telephone was installed for use at the Post Office in 1906. The bookseller's is now a chemist's and the Hotel is Ashburnham House Residential Home.

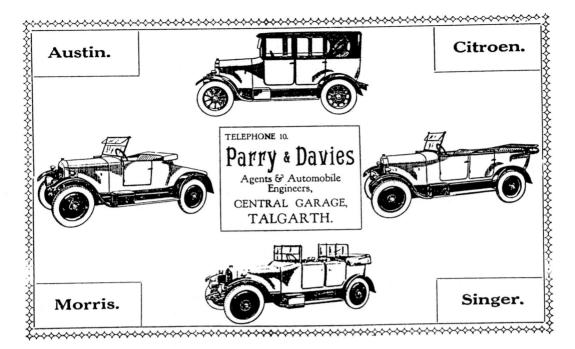

Austin.

Citroen.

TELEPHONE 10.

Parry & Davies

Agents & Automobile
Engineers,

CENTRAL GARAGE,
TALGARTH.

Morris.

Singer.

5. These are a few advertisements used by local traders many years ago although some of their names may be remembered by a few residents.

A SQUARE DEAL & GOOD SERVICE
to the Public.

For Prompt and Efficient Attention to all
MOTOR REPAIRS, 'Phone or Call

Morgan's Garage,
Regent Street, Talgarth,
'Phone 14.

AGENT for AUSTIN, DAIMLER, CLYNO,
MORRIS CARS, &c.

B.S.A., RALEIGH, RUDGE & SUNBEAM CYCLES
and MOTOR CYCLES.

DUNLOP and MICHELIN TYRE STOCKIST.

CARS FOR HIRE.

Ironmongery, General Furnishing & Hardware Department,
BELL STREET.

FRED T. MORGAN,
TALGARTH.

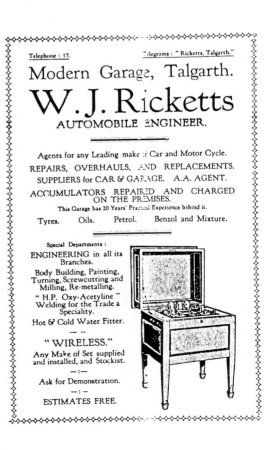

Telephone : 17.   Telegrams : " Ricketts, Talgarth."

Modern Garage, Talgarth.

W. J. Ricketts
AUTOMOBILE ENGINEER.

Agents for any Leading make of Car and Motor Cycle.

REPAIRS, OVERHAULS, AND REPLACEMENTS.

SUPPLIERS for CAR & GARAGE. A.A. AGENT.

ACCUMULATORS REPAIRED AND CHARGED
ON THE PREMISES.

This Garage has 20 Years' Practical Experience behind it.

Tyres.   Oils.   Petrol.   Benzol and Mixture.

Special Departments :
ENGINEERING in all its
Branches.
Body Building, Painting,
Turning, Screwcutting and
Milling, Re-metalling.
" H.P. Oxy-Acetyline "
Welding for the Trade a
Speciality.
Hot & Cold Water Fitter.

— —

" WIRELESS."
Any Make of Set supplied
and installed, and Stockist.

— :—

Ask for Demonstration.

— :—

ESTIMATES FREE.

6. To be seen on the Trefecca Road is the dwelling now known as Cae Post. Whilst this photograph is a little aged, the building has an even longer history as it was at one time a local toll house.

The Old Tower, Talgarth. S 1687 M.

7. A view taken from the bank of the River Enig looking at the rear of the 14th century tower. The little girl at the bottom of the steps poses for a photographer in 1904, the picture later being hand-coloured and used to produce some of the first coloured postcards to be sent from Talgarth.

8./9. Two further views from yesteryear of the Tower and Bridge. In the picture above, gone are the old trees and the War Memorial is sited near to where the 1930s model car is standing.

10. The Square at Talgarth is probably the most photographed scene in the town, being taken from all angles and yet each one usually offers something different to remember. Above, the year is about 1932 with some modern cars of the day to be seen.

11. This photograph taken from the Tower Hotel during the early 1950s, shows in the background one of Talgarth's former ecological landmarks, the elm trees. These were felled in about 1953 an event that would probably raise strong protest in these days of greater conservation.

12.   The River Enig at one time must have provided a constant supply of fresh water to the villagers at the turn of the last century. This picture from 1900 shows an old lady in the costume of the day stood with her pail on the river bank.

13. Two old stone-built cottages which were situated near the 'T' junction at the southern end of Talgarth by-pass, adjacent to the Talgarth Rugby Football Club. These were demolished in the 1960s but will no doubt be remembered by many readers of this book and also perhaps the occupants of the nearest one seen here, Mr and Mrs Collet. Also to be noticed are some remains of the railway line which ran close by.

14. Unfortunately it has not been possible to pin point the exact location of the little cottage on this photograph of a hundred years ago. It is however of an old toll house which once stood near Bronllys.

15. An old picture of some of the shops in the Square offers a good example of continuing change to the village centre.

16. A lone cyclist stands in the middle of The Green, Talgarth, a road which is very different and much busier these days. In the background can be seen 13th century Bronllys Castle.

The Green, Talgarth.

17. Another view of The Green, this time during the 1940s with considerable changes and new housing having appeared since.

18.   July 17th 1920 was a day of great excitement and celebration as Talgarth welcomed a Royal visit by their Majesties King George V, Queen Mary and Princess Mary. This is High Street in full decoration.

19. Another picture from the day of the Royal visit with some interesting slogans to be noticed.

Talgarth

20./21. Two panoramic views overlooking Talgarth from many years ago. The church is the prominent feature but many new houses have been constructed since these pictures were taken, changing the face of the area considerably. The photograph below is taken from Bronllys Castle.

GENERAL VIEW. TALGARTH

22. Some of the staff of Evans' General Stores in about 1926. The gentleman pictured on the far right and sporting a 'Dai cap' is Mr L Pugh. As to be seen in the advertisement below, there was a time when a visitor to Talgarth could enjoy a week's bed and breakfast at Evans' Commercial Hotel for a mere £3.15!

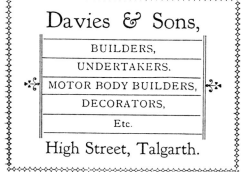

23. The year is 1939 so only the more mature residents of Talgarth are asked to recall some of the faces seen here. Edwards' delivery van is parked outside their shop with driver Ernie Griffiths accompanied by Miss I Conlin, Mr J Gwynne and the manager Mr Griffiths who was probably more often referred to as 'Griff the Enig'.

24. The Market Square as it looked in 1914 with little motor traffic to be seen, unlike today's volumes which pound the area.

25. Looking up Bell Street during the 1950s and judging by the relaxed looking dog outside the old Post Office, things were a little quieter in those days!

The Black Mountains, Talgarth. 401.

26./27. Two views of Talgarth from the past. The photograph above was taken in about 1920 and depicts a sparse scene compared with today. Below is a view some years later and is photographed overlooking the road leading to the Mid Wales Hospital.

TALGARTH FROM S.E.

28./29.   Almost 40 years separate these two views looking over the bridge towards the Square. Above, the year is 1901 to be compared with 1940 below. The Bridgend Inn still has its old ornate frontage but a public telephone kiosk has arrived near the Town Hall by 1940. The kiosk is distinctively painted white to enable identification in the dark, for these were the days of the Second World War with prolonged hours of nightly blackouts in force.

30. The white house pictured above is yet another example of a bygone building of old Talgarth. This was originally an almshouse, which was an aged system of privately supported housing offering accommodation to the elderly and needy. However, the house is seen here in later years with Mrs Wood stood in the doorway with her infant daughter Maisie. The dwelling was eventually demolished during the 1980s and is now the site of a garage.

31. Whilst it has not been possible to trace the names of the two gentlemen here, they are in fact both Talgarth residents. The scene is at one of the local farms with what appears to be a steam operated threshing machine from the 1920s or 1930s.

32. There is little visual evidence remaining in Talgarth these days that there ever was a railway system in the district. Merthyr, Newport and Hereford were all easily accessible by steam train until the devastating re-structuring of British Railways, as it was then known in the early 1960s. The tracks seen here now form the route of the by-pass but the station buildings can still be recognised after having been converted into a private dwelling.

Talgarth, Penbont.

33. A scene near Penbont Cottage on the way down from the Mid-Wales Hospital. A few changes have taken place here now with some new houses having been built on the left. Seen here are the dwellings of Viewlands and Rose Cottage.

34. Yet another facet of everyday life which appears to be on the decline is the door to door delivery of the daily 'pinta'. Mr Jim Prosser is pictured with the rather unusual delivery combination of motorcycle and side car distributing milk direct from the churn during the 1930s.

35. A photograph of a number of local advertisers who once used the side of the Bridgend Hotel as their hoarding. This picture shows the scene as it was at the outbreak of war in 1939. Amongst many emergency measures put into place, was one to remove directional road signs and station names etc. This was aimed at confusing the enemy of his whereabouts should he have landed covertly in the countryside. In this particular photograph, the name Talgarth has been carefully painted over, beneath 'W J Ricketts the Garage', and after the telephone number. If one views the side wall today, it will be seen that the details were never replaced and it looks the same today as it did almost 60 years ago.

36. A look at The Square from days before the arrival of a proper road surface and pavements. In those days it was safe enough for the two ladies to be chatting outside the Tower Hotel!

37./38. Two views from the winter of 1947. Above is the scene at Regent Street and New Road, whilst below, with Mr A Davies on the left, snow clearing is in progress near Bell's Orchard. These photographs do not totally portray the extreme weather conditions of the time, as February and March of that year brought the worst snowstorms and blizzards ever, to hit South and Mid-Wales. Declared as 'the year of the shovel', chaos ruled for weeks with road and rail transport grinding to a halt causing even worse food and fuel shortages already in force due to post war rationing.

CHAPTER 2

The Neighbouring Villages

39. Looking towards the Black Mountains from the quiet village of Bronllys in the early 1950s. The village must be regarded as an ancient and historical settlement with its medieval church and 13th century Castle remains.

40./41. Two peaceful scenes of Bronllys which indicate a few changes having taken place. Above and on the right is Vicarage Cottage, originally known as Clerk's Cottage and since demolished. Below and some twenty years on, welcome improvements to the road and pavements have been made and on the left the Post Office is to be seen.

42. What is now a busy thoroughfare through the village is pictured here in 1912 with a lone horse and cart constituting the day's traffic. In the background on the right can be seen the Cock Hotel.

43. Probably one of the most prestigious events for the village of Bronllys was the royal visit by their Majesties King George V and Queen Mary (grandparents to our present Queen) on July 17th 1920. The occasion was to perform the official opening of the newly completed South Wales Sanatorium. The picture on the left shows the welcoming decorations erected over the road leading from Talgarth into Bronllys.

44. All the equipment, ingredients and workers are available here for a cider-making session outside the Cock Hotel in about 1935.

COCK HOTEL

45. St Peter's Church, Glasbury pictured when the railway line to Hay-on-Wye ran alongside the churchyard. This church was consecrated in 1665, the original St Peter's being a short distance away, near the Wye Bridge. A great flood in 1662 engulfed this building and actually changed the course of the river. The railway line seen here was first opened in 1864 following an old tram line which was opened in 1818 to link the traffic between the Brecon Canal, Talgarth and Hay-on-Wye.

46. A view which overlooks picturesque Glasbury-on-Wye, from just above the old station. This picture is from 1903 and in the distance can be seen Maesllwch Castle still in its original design before partial demolition in 1951. The village of Glasbury dates back to the year 1055 when Gruffydd ap Llewellyn defeated Ralph, Earl of Hereford, who was a nephew of Edward the Confessor at the Battle of Glasbury.

47. The road to Hereford is carried over the River Wye by this bridge at Glasbury, this particular photograph being some fifty years old. The river bank here is a popular site for visitors during the summer months. The name of Glasbury is derived from the Welsh, Clas (a green enclosure) and A'Rwy (on the Wye).

48. Three Cocks Junction in the 1950s as a steam hauled passenger train enters the station. The station sign at the time read 'Change for Builth Wells, Llandrindod Wells, Llandiloes and the Cambrian Coast'. Today's generation will find difficulty in finding the location of this station as it is now the site of some industrial unit buildings and the Calor Gas Storage Depot.

49. Down the village at Three Cocks in the 1940s when things were a little quieter than today. On the left is the road to Builth Wells and straight on for Glasbury and Hay.

50. The Mill village shop, cafe and petrol station as it was in 1960. Looking at it today it will be noted that not all of the trees have survived but the business is still operated by Mr Doug Lewis.

51./52. The Three Cocks Hotel and Restaurant as it looked in 1905 and 1930 when the climbing ivy had taken hold. This unique and ancient building dates from the 15th century with its sign of Three Cocks dating from the Battles of Poitiers and Crecy, when a descendant of one of the deposed Welsh rulers fought under King Edward III. His service was rewarded by the King with a coat of arms - Three Cocks on a silver shield. The Hotel, standing on the Hereford to Brecon Road is a highly praised hostelry nowadays.

THE HOTEL, THREE COCKS.

Llangorse Village.

52. Just four miles (6.4 kms) from Talgarth lies the village of Llangorse and here is a scene from the end of the 19th century. On the right is today's post office next to the general store.

53. Above and seen in Edwardian times is a view overlooking the village of Llangorse with the Brecon Beacons in the distance.

54. Again pictured in the Edwardian era is Llangorse Lake, the largest natural such expanse of water in South Wales. Ever popular with tourists and water sport enthusiasts, the lake and village are abound with local fable and legend. One such tale is that the remains of an ancient castle lie beneath the waters, condemned by God in a day of wrath and divine vengeance.

55. It is 1910 and the sum total of Langorse's traffic appears to be this horse-drawn bread delivery cart which is advertising 'Hovis'.

56. The heart of the village in the 1950s with the ever popular Red Lion Hotel on the left and St Paulinus Church on the right.

57. The highly acclaimed and popular Griffin Inn at Llyswen and this is how it looked in 1959.

58. Photographed outside the Griffin are the 'Griffin Grafters'. The ladies are members of the raft team who participated in the raft race held on the River Wye from Hay to Chepstow, a gruelling event which takes three days to complete.

59. The main road through the best kept village of Llyswen at the turn of the century. The post office is on the left next to the village shop and the Star Public House further along.

Llyswen

41

60. The village of Pengenffordd lies virtually at the peak of the Crickhowell to Talgarth Road. The ancient Castle Inn is still there although regulars will soon recognise a few exterior changes since this picture was taken.

61. Here are a few Pengenffordd villagers of yesteryear. On the left is Mr David Jones one time landlord of the Castle who brewed his own beer at the pub. He died in 1947 at the ripe old age of ninety-five. In the centre is his wife Sarah who was the local midwife and on the right, in old Welsh Victorian attire is Mr Jones' mother pictured at the Castle.

CHAPTER 3

Historic Buildings

Tregunter (Talgarth)

62. The Rise and Fall of Tregunter Park

Tregunter was originally called Gunterstone, which dates back to the Norman Conquest of Breconshire by Bernard Newmarch. His first care was to reward his Commanders who assisted him in his conquest by sharing amongst them territories he had acquired, for example, he gave to Sir Peter Gunter the manor (land) thus - Tregunter (home of Gunter).

In 1765 Mrs I T Greenly of Titley, Herefordshire, sold the property to the second eldest of three brothers, Joseph the senior and Howell, the youngest. Thomas left home in 1727 to become a travelling tailor after serving his apprenticeship with his uncle in Llangorse. He then worked for a year or so under Joshua Pegler in Bath. By 1732 he became a master tailor in Red Lion Square but, being given to wine drinking and squandering money, he became bankrupt and left for Paris. He returned to London to start afresh and, by a stroke of good fortune, he became a regimental tailor and amassed sufficient wealth to buy Trefecca and Tregunter estates and built Tregunter Mansion. He retired on £1,000 a year in 1765.

To Tregunter came the beautiful Mary Robinson, known as 'Perdita'. She was sponsored by David Garrick befriended by Sheridan and the Duchess of Devonshire. Her portrait had been painted by several artists including Gainsborough and Joshua Reynolds and in 1774 she came as the newly married wife of the son of Thomas Harris, who had won her by intimating that he was heir to a vast estate in Wales, not telling her that he had many creditors at his heels. She left her husband and the stage and became the mistress of the Prince of Wales for two short years, after which she was left with an annuity of £500 to meet her debts of £7,000.

Howell Harris, born in 1714, made Trefecca famous, for he was a teacher, preacher, reformer, agriculturist and soldier. Joseph and Howell invented new methods which enabled the implementation of the Industrial Revolution in Wales. They were also the founders of the Breconshire Agricultural Society in 1755, the first of its kind in Wales, in fact, the first in Britain. Howell died in 1773 and was buried in Talgarth Church near the altar where he was converted. Joseph Harris was the most gifted of the three. Mathematician, inventor of scientific instruments, an authority on navigation, astronomy and geography. Unfortunately, he was a very modest man and was not given the honour he so richly deserved. In 1736 he was the Assay Master in the Royal Mint with his residence in the Tower. He died in 1764 and was buried in the Tower of London.

The mansion at Tregunter that Thomas Harris built was set in 173 acres, it had three storeys, flanked by three wings of two storeys. Thomas died in 1782 and was buried in Talgarth churchyard.

In his will, he left all his wealth to his niece, Joseph's only daughter, Anna Maria, who married a Samuel Hughes. They had four children, three of whom died at a very early age. The fourth, Eliza Anna, who died in 1859, married Roderick Gwynne of Buckland in 1804. He died in 1808 and in 1818 she remarried William Alexander Maddocks, who was a rich altruist and spent ten years in rescuing 2,000 acres of submerged salt marshes and, on the flats close to the cliffs he built an entire model town, Tremadoc, which was named after him. Their daughter Eliza Anne Ermine, married John Webb Roche of Rochemount, Co Cork, Ireland in 1851 and resided at the Tregunter estate. William Maddocks went bankrupt and died in exile in Paris and his wife remained in residence at Tregunter.

On his death, John Webb Roche was buried near the west gate in Talgarth churchyard and on his ornate and prodigious vault there is the following inscription:- 'Here repose the remains of John Webb Roche of Rochemount, Co Cork, Ireland and of Tregunter Park, Breconshire, who departed this life January 6th 1869.'

His son was born Francis William Alexander in 1854, who inherited the estate from his grandmother and he married Ellen Beatrice de Winton.

In 1856 the Roche family was granted an Irish peerage, the first being Edmund Burke Roche, born 1815. The late Lord Fermoy, who was the fifth baron, Edmund James Burke Roche (whose father inherited the Tremadoc Estate) was a brother to Frances Ruth Burke Roche, mother of the present Princess of Wales. The coat of arms of the late Lord Fermoy consists of three fish (roach), with a lion on one side and a greyhound on the other, with a sea eagle or osprey on the crest. The coat of arms of John Webb Roche, which can be seen on his vault is very similar.

In Brecon Cathedral a small door leads to the sacristy which was the Tregunter Chapel up to the turn of the century and there are several monuments to be seen here.

In 1859 the 21st Breconshire Battalion was created and after a number of years, six companies were formed, and F Company (Talgarth) being the last. In 1881 it was changed to the 1st Volunteer Battalion South Wales Borderers I VB SWB Headquarters, Wharf House, Brecon. In 1872, FWA Roche joined to become in 1896, Lt Colonel. He died in 1897 at the age of 43. In Talgarth Church on the east window is inscribed - 'To the Glory of God and in Memory of Francis William Alexander Roche of Tregunter, Colonel of Breconshire Volunteers. (Died 8th August, 1897, age 43 years). Mrs Roche had the Drill Hall, Talgarth (now Joe's Lodge) built in memory of her husband in 1900.

In the service of the Colonel was Tom Crane. He was first coachman and his preference was to drive the Colonel and, secondly, Mrs Roche. Tom Crane with many others had the arduous task of transporting the first patients to the Mid-Wales Hospital in 1904 from Pen-y-Val Hospital, Abergavenny.

The new tenure of Tregunter Estate was Captain Hughes Morgan, later to become Sir David Hughes Morgan, who died in Pennally, Pembrokeshire. He was educated at Queen's College, Oxford and he became a solicitor and Justice of the Peace. He was a donor of funds for scholarships at Christ College, Brecon, and appointed a Governor; he joined the Breconshire and Radnorshire Militia (3rd Batt) SWB. He retired as Captain and subsequently joined the Breconshire Volunteers.

Captain Hughes Morgan was a very charitable benevolent gentleman to say the least, he was always at hand to those in need for, at Christmas the Town Hall at Talgarth was stocked with provisions of all description for the needy and under-privileged of the district.

He owned the first car registered in Breconshire, registration number EU 1 and, as was customary in the early days of motoring, a member of his staff proceeded in front of his car with a red flag. His chauffeur was Mr Fred Evans of the Swan Hotel, Talgarth, who had the honour of being the chauffeur to Dr Randall Davidson, the Archbishop of Canterbury on his tour of Carmarthen in 1907. The Captain was a keen sportsman and had a cricket square laid in the park and this was later to become a third green of Talgarth Golf Club in 1919.

The Gordon family took ownership about 1910 and put the property up for sale in 1916. The estate was sold in two lots, the 173 acres of land were purchased by Mr D P Hopkins of Bronllys. Mrs Gordon moved to Devon and sold the mansion piecemeal, for example, tapestries and a remarkable staircase were shipped to America. Parts of the mansion were taken to Devon and the remainder of the house was demolished by Messrs T D Evans and Sons of Tower Shop Talgarth about 1923/24.

The remnants of the mansion were used for the foundations of the Talgarth mart and the terrace steps and railings for the new entrance to the Talgarth Town Hall in 1926.

Tregunter Park was unique in many respects and still is in many ways. It had a great variety of trees, ie Hornbeam, Wellingtonia, Beechwood, American Redwood, Scotch Firs, all types of Acacia and Monkey Puzzle trees, to name just a few. During the First World War the mansion housed German POWs who worked in farms in the district during the day.

All that remains today of this immense estate are the three dog kennels and the stables for the working horses. There were hackney stables but only a small portion remains and on one wall a few ornate ceramic tiles can still be seen.

63. Tom Crane, head coachman to the Roche family.

44

64./65. Two distinctive yesteryear views of St Gwendoline's Church, Talgarth whose origins date back to the thirteenth century. It is likely therefore that the church and its grounds formed the dwelling places of Talgarth's earliest inhabitants in the age of Celtic Saints. The interior of this church is full of splendour and classic design and the remains of founder Methodist, Howell Harris are interred in front of the altar rails. As always, buildings of this age and grandeur are in constant need of repair and funding is most welcome. The present vicar is Rev David Trevor Walters.

66. A picture taken of Bethlehem Chapel in Talgarth in the year 1900. This church has been a place of worship in the village since its opening in 1880.

67. Penuel Baptist Chapel which has stood in the heart of Llangorse village since the year 1869. Unfortunately irreversible declines in attendances enforced final closure of this place of worship in 1996.

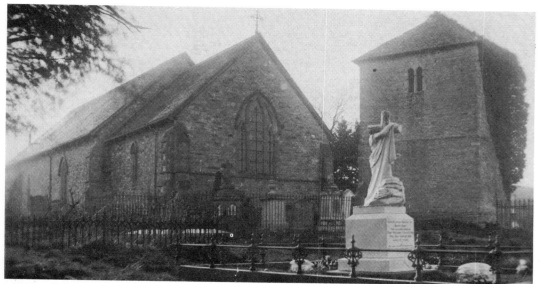

68. St Mary's Church Bronllys pictured in the 1920s. There has been a place of worship on this site since medieval times but the present church is one of complete restoration which took place in 1889 following a state of serious disrepair. The new church in its Norman style was rebuilt on the same ground plan as the original building, with the base of the old walls being retained. Interesting features include the separate bell tower which survives from the original church construction and a font which dates back to the fourteenth century. Visitors to the church these days will also note the absence of the railings surrounding many of the graves on this photograph. The metal was removed during World War Two to be re-cycled for more urgent military use at the time.

69. Some two and a half miles from Talgarth lies the 13th century church of Llaneleu, within its circular churchyard which suggests as at St Gwendolines Talgarth, that the area was the containment of the earliest members of the community. There are several examples of ancient worship here including several Celtic Crosses and the roof turret contains an original bell believed to have been cast by the monks of Llanthony.

70. The bell-ringers of Bronllys Church pictured in 1943 and some of the names recalled are left to right, back row - D Price, P Paterson, R Hill, F Rouse, W Bevan, D Bennet and E Drew. Included in the front are Rev Davies, R Turner, F Turner and D Owens.

71. Llangorse Church was founded in the sixth century by St Paulinus who settled in the village from Llandeusant and established a local monastery. The interior design of the present church suggests a construction belonging to the fifteenth or sixteenth century, much of the roof supports being original. Archaeologists have identified numerous relics and burials dating to the eighth century. Steeped in history the church font is 700 years old and the organ is a masterpiece from 1674 and still in use today, originating from St Johns, Cardiff having been acquired by Llangorse in 1898. The incumbent is currently Rev Rowland T Edwards with assistant curate Rev Michael Edwards.

72./73. Pleasantly situated just two miles from Talgarth is the little village of Llanfilo, with its parish church of St Bilo within the diocease of Swansea and Brecon. Above is a modern-day photograph whilst below, the interior is seen many years before. There are numerous gravestones in the grounds dating to the eighteenth century and an interesting lych gate with the following inscription. 'This lych gate was repaired to the greater glory of God and grateful remembrance of the men of Llanfilo William James Jones, Everard David Phillips and William John Powell who gave their lives in the Great War 1914-1918.'

74./75. Trevecca College and the Memorial Chapel. The chapel was opened in 1873 to mark the centenary of the death of Howell Harris the celebrated leader of Methodism in the area during the eighteenth century. Trevecca Theological College was founded in 1868 by the Countess of Huntingdon who was known as the Queen of Methodists. The chapel now houses a small museum dedicated to the Harris family and the picture below has changed significantly in that the chapel spire has been removed and more modern buildings have been constructed in the grounds.

Wernos, near Llyswen, Home of Howel Harris's First Methodist Society 1787.

76. Howell Harris (1714-1773), embroiled in the great Methodist revival of the early eighteenth century rallied the local population to the cause and founded a Methodist community which he called 'The Family'. The followers occupying themselves in the agricultural and rural industries of the district. The photograph above is of Wernos, near Llyswen where the first local Methodist society was formed.

77. Close to Talgarth is centuries-old Gwernyfed Mansion where King Charles I wined and dined during his travels through Wales in 1645. Built around 1600, this particular photograph is from 1904 and shows the ivy-clad left-hand side of the house which was destroyed by fire in the 1940s and never repaired. The mansion is now a Grade 1 listed building and is more recognised as the Gwernyfed Country Manor Hotel.

78. A close-up view of Maesllwch Castle of Glasbury in its original form. Maesllwch, which means Dusty Meadow was completed in 1829 and is now privately owned.

79. The original mansion of Tregoyd was built in the fourteenth century by Humphrey de Bohun, Earl of Hereford, later passing into the possession of the Gunter family during the reign of Edward VI. Records indicate Tregoyd Manor as being separated into two distinct portions in the sixteenth century with the mention 'William Gunter and Thomas ap Thomas Walter holdeth halve a knighte's fee in Tregoide.' Obviously by design, the building seen above is not the original structure, as that was destroyed by fire to be replaced by a new house on the same site. The house and estate are now owned by Sir Martin Evans-Bevan and serve as an adventure centre with a wide variety of outdoor pursuits catering for children of all ages.

80. A picture-postcard illustrating various views of the South Wales Sanatorium during the 1940s.

The Nurses' Quarters
Talgarth Sanitorium. 567.

81./82. Plans for a sanatorium to be used for the treatment of sufferers of tuberculosis were first discussed in the Talgarth area in 1913. However, due to funding and the interruptions of World War One, the complex was not finally opened until March 1920. Generous donations in appreciation of the hospital's work enabled many extensions and improvements in ensuing years such as a chapel, recreation hall and numerous medical units. The introduction of new drugs during the 1940s and 1950s plus the gradual eradication of the disease, changed the role of the hospital completely. These days the care is given more to the elderly and those requiring recuperation. These two photographs are approximately sixty years old and show just a few of the buildings.

Chalets - Sanatorium, Talgarth.

83. The expanse of the hospital and the estate are exemplified in this photograph taken from the air in about 1954. Note the Mansion House in the top left hand corner where the hospital first began in 1913.

Pontywall Sanatorium.

84. Pontywal Mansion as it was originally known was converted into a sanatorium in 1913. The premises are currently used as the headquarters of Powys Health Authority before their impending transfer which will leave an uncertain future for this old house yet again. The grounds in front of Pontywal have changed considerably over the years.

85. Originally called the Brecon and Radnor Joint Asylum on opening in 1903, the name was changed in 1921 to the Mid-Wales Hospital. This complex was built on an estate of 261 acres known as Chancefield. It is believed that the major reason why this site was chosen at Talgarth in preference to one recommended at Three Cocks, was primarily the easy availability of supplies of local stone for the construction. Also close at hand, was a regular supply of good quality water from the nearby Pwll-y-Wrach waterfall which was to be fed by gravity into the hospital's own reservoir. This system actually remained in use until about 1970 before the supply was provided by the Water Board.

The first patients at the hospital were admissions mainly from the Brecon area but numbers also arrived from towns further afield such as Swansea and Shrewsbury. Initially intended to cater for three hundred and fifty two patients, at one point at the end of 1925 there were four hundred and fifty-five, stretching resources to the limit. Some of this overcrowding was attributed to World War One and the effect that was to have, on many men who served in the battles. Consequently Wards East 7 and 8 and an X-ray Department were added to cope with the increased demands. The hospital had numerous resources of its own, such as a working farm until 1955 and the generation of its own electricity until 1961, such was the importance of the 'Mid-Wales'. Some 155 acres of farmland however were sold in 1957 and 27 acres of Pwll-y-Wrach dingle transferred to the Forestry Commission. A number of improvements were completed during the next twenty years such as a new treatment block in 1965 and an Occupational/Industrial Therapy Department in 1971. In 1974 the Powys Health Authority came into being assuming control, with matters changing again in 1993 with the formation of the Powys (NHS) Trust. Policy changes by government in recent years have indicated that the return of the mentally unfortunate to the community wherever possible would be advantageous, thus inevitably the need for such institutions as the Mid-Wales has declined drastically. At the time of publication of this book it is believed that the hospital will close for good in 1998 with some facilities being combined with nearby Bronllys.

CHAPTER 4

People and Events

86. 1951 saw the Festival of Britain with celebratory carnivals being held around the country. This entry at Talgarth was entitled 'Nursery Rhymes' and the children are, left to right, back row - R B James, S Hart, M Watkins, L Prosser, T Hughes, T Evans, M Watkins, D Crane and O Miles. Front - E Miles and J Davies.

87. From 1937 when horsedrawn traffic was common sight, is this photograph taken at the rear of Bronllys Post Office. Seated on the right is Vanny Watkins, niece of T Watkins who kept the post office and shop in Bronllys.

88. The sport of 'trotting' is very popular in Mid-Wales however on this occasion donkeys are doing the pulling instead of horses at this Donkey Derby in 1970.

89. A carnival float with the theme 'Pans People' decked with some familiar Talgarth faces in 1973. Seen left to right are Austin Davies the DJ and and the girls are Christine Prosser, Mary Davies, Pauline Davies, Rita Jones and Pat Powell.

90. The ladies of Talgarth at a 1937 carnival and amongst the faces are, at the front Misses Irene Conlin and Megan Williams, included behind are D Price and G Evans. The queen on this occasion was a lady from Hay-on-Wye.

91. This carnival photograph which was taken at Talgarth just a few weeks before the outbreak of World War Two includes some once familiar faces such as Mr Dai Williams and Mr Peter Prosser.

92. Some prizegiving is in progress at the 1937 Talgarth Carnival and some faces to be remembered are Miss Conlin, Miss M Williams and Miss G Evans.

93. Unfortunately the author has been unable to trace the precise details of this photograph so readers are asked to try and identify for themselves. It is probably another picture from a 1930s Talgarth Carnival event.

94. These smiling ladies belong to the Talgarth Women's Institute which was formed in 1922. This is one of their earliest photographs and there are plenty of faces to identify. Some of those seen include, back row - Mrs Fawke, Mrs C Davies, Miss F Morris, Mrs 'Sid' Hughes and Mrs M Weston. Third row - Mrs M Davies, Mrs S Moses and three schoolteachers who may be remembered, Miss Maggie Lewis, Miss Ashton and Miss Davies. Second row - Mrs Skyrme, Mrs Wyndham Davies, Mrs Jayne (W I President), Miss Cissie Morgan, Mrs 'Fred Parry' and Mrs Cadwalader. Front row - Mrs Scadding, Freda Hughes, Eileen Davies and Miss Lena Davies.

95. From the 1920s the workers at Gwyrne Fawr Water Works are pictured here. Not all the names can be recalled but here are a few, back row, left to right - unknown, Josh Wood, Jim Mitchell (Senior), Jim Pugh, F Pritchard, unknown, Jim Mitchell (Junior) and R Harper. Middle row - unknown, unknown, D Watkins, unknown, D Lewis, unknown and P James. Front row - A Davies, W Bridewell, unknown, unknown, unknown, G Havard and Edmund Lewis.

96. Talgarth's Fire Brigade was first formed in the year 1907 with a horsedrawn tender. Here, many years later, in 1959 are the members of the joint Brecon and Radnor Fire Service and left to right are - R Pugh, T Williams, D Davies, W Lloyd, J Price, O Havard, E Morgan, C Richards, J Jones, L Hart and P Havard.

97. Even further up to date are these members of the Powys Fire Service. Seen here are, back row - S Weale, P Blackwell, G Davies, G Hatton, R Williams and B Reid. Front row - B Coles, A Morris, B Davies and N Wilson.

98./99. Both of these photographs taken on May 8th 1995 re-create the atmosphere felt in Talgarth during the same period in 1945 when victory in Europe towards the end of the Second World War was declared VE Day. The 50th anniversary celebrations are in full swing and the four ladies seen above, sat outside the Town Hall enjoying the event are left to right, Mrs Machin, Mrs Bayliss, Miss G I Davies and Mrs Thompson.

100. 1957 and a service is being held to mark the dedication of the new war memorial at Talgarth with Rev Gurnos Davies in attendance. The original memorial was placed in the Town Hall but the positioning of this was heavily criticised for many years until agreement was finally reached to choose the site above. Locals will note that the memorial itself has been altered slightly since.

101. In 1957 the honour of 'Best Kept Village in Breconshire' went to Bronllys and here are some of the villagers facing the camera at the time. V T Williams, T Weale, D Owen, H Evans, T P Curtis, Tudor Watkins and E Weale.

102. Talgarth WI in 1962 and a host of faces to be seen. The author apologises to those not recognised but here are a few names to be remembered, back row Mrs George. Fourth row - Mrs C Morgan, Mrs Lewis and Mrs G Jones. Third row - Mrs Lewis, Mrs D Watton, Mrs D Jones, Mrs E Davies, Mrs R G Davies, Miss L Davies, Mrs Fawke, Mrs Owen and Mrs James. Second row - Mrs J Turner, Mrs Powell, Mrs Bryant, Mrs P Jones, Mrs Woodyatt, Mrs D Williams, Mrs Davies, Mrs O Edwards, Mrs F Moses and Mrs S Moses. Seated - Mr Weale (Treasurer), Mrs Islwyn Davies, Miss Morris, Mrs Cadwalader, Mrs Williams and Mrs George.

103. This time the year is 1950 and the WI are pictured sporting their banner. In the back row are - E Davies, unknown, A Druro, A Price, H Bennett, D Williams and Mrs Fred Morgan. Middle row - Mrs Williams, Mrs Dai Jones (Flossie Moses), Miss Cissie Morgan, Mrs Bryant and M Hopkins. Front row - Mrs Olive Edwards, unknown, unknown, Mrs Jack Jones and Mrs Mitchell.

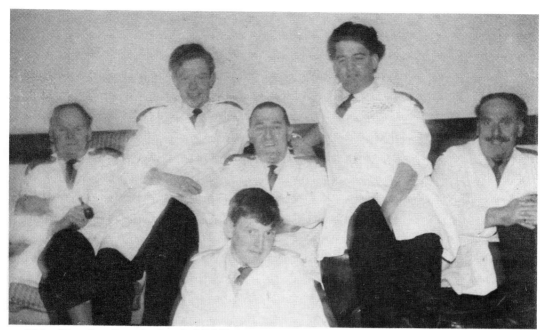

104. Time for a 'breather' at the Mid-Wales Hospital and here are a few of the male nurses. In the front is David Lewis and at the back left to right are O Davies, B Devereux, R Lewis, P Williams and T Reardon.

105. Some members of staff at the Mid-Wales in 1964. In the back row are - S Davies, S Parry, M Lewis, D Jones, G Lewis, N Pugh, J Parry, S Price and C Davies. Seated are - E Hinchcliffe, R Scott, J Davies, G I Davies, Matron Mawr, O Davies, S Pugh, R Tanswell and M Pugh.

106.   It is not certain when this photograph was taken but the crowds are at the tables for a New Year's Eve dinner at the Mid-Wales.

107. Christmas Day is not a rest period at the Mid-Wales as witnessed by the staff here during Christmas 1952 and amongst those to be seen are Matron Mawr, Mr Jones, B Haines, Jim Weale (Head Chef), G Humphreys, Mrs Vaughan, Jean Crane and Laura Davies.

108. This is a photograph taken outside the hospital in about 1934 and most of the gentlemen have been identified. Back row - W Brace, I Pugh, T Brace and D Reardon. Middle row - C Williams, A Giles, C Howell and T Jones. Front row - Two gents on the right are Messrs E Evans and R Lewis.

109. These smiling faces belong to the hospital's laundry staff who have found a few minutes spare time at the hospital to have their photograph taken. Apologies to the lady at the front left whose name has been untraceable. However, standing at the rear is Mrs E Jones with Mrs Edwards whilst at the front are Mrs W Morgan and Mrs Humphreys.

110. Ladies' fashions including nursing uniforms have advanced considerably since this picture was taken! The year is 1923 and one member of staff positively identified at the Mid-Wales is Mrs A Williams who is third form the left.

111. A photograph from yesteryear is that of Mr Thomas holding a 'Phillip and Mary', a strange name given locally to an old fashioned implement used in threshing. The short piece of wood tied to the long handle was called the 'swingle'.

A 'bolting' of straw would be spread out on the barn floor and the swingle would be brought down sharply and repeatedly on the straw which would be turned over and the beating continued. Finally the straw was shaken, when the grain still remaining in the 'heads' fell to the floor. It was not as easy to operate as it might appear as there was a certain skill in being able to bring the swingle down parallel to the floor to save effort on what could be a long and strenuous job down at the farm.

112. At the end of a day's threshing on this occasion by mechanical means, liquid refreshment still appears to be very welcomed. Two of the lads seen here are Messrs A Mitchell and B Haines.

113. Two locals seen relaxing with a cup of tea are Mr Crad Jones of Pendre and Trevor Davies of the old Post Office, Talgarth.

114. A patch of faultless furrows are seen here as Mr Crad Jones is pictured winning the county ploughing match.

115. An exceptionally old photograph which was taken outside the busy wheelwright's shop which once stood on ground opposite today's public house, the New Inn. Automation naturally brought the ancient trade of the wheelwright to a close and this picture dates from about 1895.

116. A scene near the old Post Office at Bronllys in 1923. Notice the old horse trough which was still in use while cider making was carried out at the Cock Hotel.

117. A multitude of potato pickers take a rest after a day's crop digging in the fields of Talgarth.

118. Here is a gang of potato pickers from Talgarth and the surrounding area and sat on the old Fordson tractor is Mrs Fred Morgan. Among those on the trailer, left to right are D Mitchell, H Evans, Mr Norman (Trevecca Road), S Giles, F Bentley, Mr Evans, G Hughes, M Weale, E Griffiths, Aggie (The Swan), Mrs Sid Evans, Mrs Hughes, Mrs Gwillian (The Cwm), Mrs Speake, Mrs Humphries and Mrs Barnes.

119. Celebrations and presentations are under way at the Castle Hotel Talgarth when money raised at an auction of harvest festival produce was distributed to worthy causes. Councillor Harry Evans presented £700 to Mrs D Jones of Usk House and Mr J Rosewell presented £300 to Mary Fellows of 'Dial-a-Ride'. On the photograph are Mrs J Rosewell, Mr P Haines, Mrs D Jones, Councillor H Evans, Mr J Rosewell, Mary Fellows, Mr M Jones, Miss N Davies, Valerie Heath, Mr B Davies and Mrs Jean Chinnery.

120. The cooks and helpers who provided so well for the Luncheon Club at Christmas 1995 include the following - Mrs Hart, Mrs Hawker, Mrs Smart, Mrs Harvey, Nona Davies, Mrs Knapp, Mrs S Williams, Mrs Powell, Mrs Watton, Mrs Kite, Mrs Lewis, Tom Berry and Mr Prosser.

121. A good photograph to reminisce with, is this one of a group of Talgarth folk possibly on a day's outing in the 1940s. Regrettably just a few names are recalled by the author but in the back left is Miss Griffiths and on the right in Mr Collet. In the front are Mrs Poole, Mrs Powell, Mrs Wood and Mrs Collet.

122. The Christmas Dinner is in progress by the Luncheon Club at Talgarth's Town Hall. Some of the guests are Mr and Mrs Prosser on the right and far left is Mr Tom Williams.

123. All important in past days of labour shortage, particularly during wartime was the Land Army, the girls performing many arduos duties on the farms to maintain food supplies etc. This group of ladies was stationed at Talgarth during the 1940s and early 1950s and two of them were to remain in the village and marry local boys. The lady at the top left married Mr D Price and the lady on the far right became Mrs Harvey Evans.

124. An anniversary celebration by the Women's Institute. At the back are Mrs Coppin, Mrs Plunkett, Mrs Hart and Mrs Druro. In the front row are Mrs Cadwallader, Mrs D Lewis, Mrs F Moses, Mrs Fawke, Mrs Humphreys, Mrs Lewis, Mrs I Davies, Mrs J Turner, Mrs James and Mrs Mitchell.

125. Pictured at a nursing exhibition which was held at Brecon in 1960 are among others, E James, A Price, Matron Mawr, D Reardon, E Reardon, A Lewis and T Allen.

126. Students and their theologian mentors pose for the photographer on their last day of training at Trevecca College in June 1906. Photographs such as these were often reproduced as picture postcards and sold as greetings cards.

127. Talgarth Male Voice Choir pictured before leaving for the Royal Albert Hall to attend the 'One Thousand Voices Festival' in 1983. Back row, left to right - Len Davies, unknown, Dai Timothy, Steve Davies, Elwyn Davies, Brychan Davies, Bill Symmonds, Tommy Pugh, Dai Phillips, Laurie Butcher and Les King. Third row - 'Bob' Davies, Tony Evans, Bob Meredith, Peter Pugh, Nigel Keylock, unknown, Roy Davies, John Edwards, unknown, Laurie Price, Mike Ford, Gerry Bastin and Roy Evans. Second row - Idris Jones, Joe Parry, Ted Fawke, Idris Davies, Gron Jones, John Jones, Ken Rees, Dick Price, David Hughes, John Thomas, Ernie James and Jimmy Smith. Front row - Cliff Watkins, John Crane, Steve Evans, Norman Pugh, Howard Jones, Gwyn Lewis, Albert Price, Jack Williams, Davy Jones, G B Jones, Howey Jones and 'Crad' Williams. Also part of the choir but not in the picture are Mrs Morwen Pugh (Conductor) and Mrs Meg Griffiths (Accompanist).

79

128. As this book is intended to give a pictorial view of Talgarth and its people for future reference, here are two faces to be recognised. Messrs Vernon Meredith and Henry Morris.

129. The art of good cider-making receives careful attention from Bryn Haines and Bert Carey with a typical cider press seen on the right.

130. On the left is Mr Gwyn Jones pictured during a cider-making session at the New Inn in 1952 and on the right is the landlord at the time, Mr Davies.

131. On the left is Mrs Coslett, affectionately known locally as 'Granny Coslett' who lived into her nineties. Born in the 1840s she first lived at College Terrace, Trevecca then at Cliff Terrace, Talgarth. Widowed very young, after just one year of marriage and losing most of what money she had in a company failure, she turned her attentions to helping others for the rest of her life. She became a deeply religious woman who though in dire need herself, gave everything she had to deserving causes, often she received money anonymously through the post from people who pitied her but with great delight, she would decide which needy cause she would aid with these gifts from providence. She used to have visions and one she often related, was when she was feeling frightened one night whilst at home alone in Cliff Terrace, with a howling wind outside. She was making her way to bed holding her candle, being petrified of the dark when the room suddenly lit up and she saw Christ standing there telling her not to be afraid anymore. The newspapers of the 1930s described her as 'a wonderful old Welsh lady living in a village called Talgarth who professed a life of total self sacrifice.'

132. Talgarth Carnival in 1937 and the young lady with the bicycle is Rae Williams. A few more faces to be spotted are D Price, I Conlin, M Williams and G Evans.

133. The precise year is unsure but this is another Talgarth Carnival picture and no doubt there are a number of children seen here who will now be of adult age and reading this book.

134. The team of bell ringers at Talgarth Church in the year 1902 when Rev D Lewis Davies was vicar. On a heavier note, the church tower contains six bells these being installed in the year 1724.

135. Members of Bronllys Church Choir in 1954 when they were honoured with a visit by Rt Rev Glyn Simon, Bishop of Swansea and Brecon. Back row, left to right - Ivor Morris, Jennifer Blackwell, Ann Little, Rosemary Davies, Valerie Wilkinson, G Thomas (Headmaster Bronllys School), Ann Davies, Carol Millington, Beryl Morris, Dorothy Davies and Trevor Mills. Middle row - Mrs Hopkins, David Murphy, David Davies, Derek Owens, Glyn Simon (Bishop of Swansea and Brecon), Rev J Davies (Vicar of Bronllys), Robert Turner, Dennis Kenchington, Tony Millington and Mrs Davies. Front row - Marilyn Murphy, Brian Evans, Billy Millington, Tony Latham, David Davies, Nigel Kenchington, David Latham, Tyrone Davies, Terry Blackwell and Margaret Davies.

136. The crowds of adults and children dressed in the fashion of the day celebrate the opening of Llyswen Hall in December 1910.

137. Members of the first mime performed in Breconshire and two of the 'stars' are identified, third from the left is E Davies (Lewis) and far right is S Evans (Moses).

138. Two old warriors of Talgarth whilst serving in the 1st Volunteer Battalion South Wales Borderers in 1900. On the left is Mr Cuddigan who also held the prestigious position of head gardener at Tregunter Mansion and on the right is Mr T Davies (Tom the runner) a champion athlete of Talgarth. His son 'Chappie' was to follow in the sporting footsteps in playing football for Wales.

The Talgarth Volunteers

The Talgarth Volunteers were formed soon after 1859 when there seemed to be a renewed possibility of invasion. At this time it was decided that if volunteers would equip themselves with uniform and arms, and provide military instructors at their own expense the state would accept their services.

By 1888 the volunteers were organised in district brigades. The men not only provided their own uniform, they paid the salaries of some of the instructors when required and paid the rent of rooms in which they met. Slowly the character of the movement changed, it came to be regarded mainly as working class as regards the rank and file. Naturally those who were ordinary manual workers could not be expected to provide their own uniform. From this time uniforms were supplied and the expenses of the corps were met by the provision of a grant which was given on condition that efficiency would be maintained. In 1886 every volunteer rifleman was provided with a great-coat, water-bottle, haversack and means of carrying a supply of ammunition. As early as 1884 Breconshire had one of the largest volunteer battalions in the country, the Commanding Officer at this time being Colonel Gwynne of Talgarth who was often referred to as 'the father of the Volunteer movement in Breconshire'. In 1883 the Talgarth Company mustered IOC men whose activities included camping, marching, shooting and drilling. Monthly shooting contests were held and an annual competition was eagerly looked forward to, not only for the shooting but also because it ended in the Annual Dinner.

From 1870 to 1877, with the exception of one year, the Volunteers camped annually at Rhos fach Common near Talgarth but owing to it being a difficult place to get to it was resolved to change the place of rendezvous to Cefn Moel.

In 1907 fundamental changes in organisation took place. The Volunteers were remodelled into a defence force under the title of the Territorial Force.

Enlistment was for a period of four years, the age limits being seventeen and thirty five. Camps were held between May 1st and September 30th and men attended these for a period of training, usually for a fortnight.

Talgarth men were as loyal to the Territorials as they were to the old force and at the out-break of the Great War the town and parish supplied men for the F Company of the 1st Brecknocks Battalion. The F Company entrained at Talgarth Station on the 6th August, 1914, on their way to Pembroke Dock.

Their rifle training was done at Tenby with the South Wales Borderers. Most of the men of the Breconshire Territorials were in camp when war broke out and they immediately returned to Brecon. The commanding officer was Lord Glanusk, an old Grenadier officer who was adjutant of the CIVs in the Boer War. Lord Glanusk had visited Talgarth on a recruiting campaign and the Breconshire Territorials had the distinction of being the first battalion to reach its full establishment under Viscount Haldane's scheme.

On the 29th October 1914 the Battalion sailed from Southampton on the troopship Delwara. It was later reported that the ship had gone down in the Bay of Biscay. The rumour caused great alarm in Talgarth but the only trouble the ship had was a fire in the hold and some difficulty because of sea-sickness. Five days were spent at Gibraltar for repairs before the ship proceeded to Aden where the men spent eleven months. When the Armistice was signed they were at Ker Kut and it was not until the 29th March 1919 that they returned to Talgarth.

Not all the men returned and the Roll of Honour for the Town records the names of twenty-five who were killed in action. A memorial was put up in the Town Hall but due to some criticism of the suitability of the place chosen, a new memorial was erected on the bank of the Enig in 1957 in honour of the men of the two World Wars.

139. Members of Talgarth Parish Council in 1927 who appear to be wearing rosettes and displaying a trophy for some event. Seen left to right, back row - Frank Price, Vin Davies, Taffy Jones, Jenkin Evans, Sid Hughes and C Price. Middle row - Bob Davies, John Pritchard, W T Davies, Edgar Hughes, Johnny Pugh and W T Davies. Front row - S M Green, Tommy Lewis and G Brooks. Mr W T Davies was headmaster at the local school to be succeeded by Charlie Price.

140. Seen on the left is Talgarth's Mrs Bennett being interviewed by Frank Hennesy and Ray Gravell during a visit to the village by BBC Radio Wales in 1993. Mrs Bennett and Mrs Bowen are two of the most senior citizens of Talgarth and can look forward to a congratulatory telegram from Buckingham Palace in the not too distant future.

141. The fifty-one voices of Talgarth Male Voice Choir with their conductor Morwen Pugh and accompanist Meg Griffiths.

142. Pictured in the Town Hall in 1952 are more than fifty members of the Talgarth community, thought to be at a function held by the local Women's League.

143. Talgarth Carnival 1977 and here are a few participants in the 'Pancake Race'. Back row - S Lewis, N Mytton, A Jones, J Evans, P Gwillim, I Lewis, Major Green and D Morgan with the football. Middle row - C Gwillym, N Weale, A Hughes, P Jones, D Gwillym and J Hughes. Front row - W Reeves, A Jones, T Bartlett, J Evans, S Vaughan, V Weale and A Cooper.

144. Talgarth WI 1952. Back row - Mrs Carey, Mrs E Hughes, Mrs Weke, Mrs Harper, Mrs C Williams and Mrs D Jones. Middle row - Mrs Evans, Mrs Reardon, Mrs D Jones, Mrs M Thomas, Mrs E Hughes and Mrs Morris. Front row - Mrs Hinchcliffe, Mrs Moore, Mrs R Hart, Reverend and Mrs Thomas (and daughter), Mrs F Scadding and Mrs O Price.

145. Residents of Glanenig Residential Home are spending a day on the Square in Talgarth during the VE Day Anniversary celebrations May 1995, the ladies seated are Mrs A Pritchard, Mrs Wainwright, Mrs I Stephens, Mrs D Jones and Mrs C Prosser. Standing behind are Mrs Jones, Matron M Bowen, Mrs P Thompson and Mrs Kite (Members of the staff).

146. Some local running enthusiasts on a fund-raising event thought to be collecting for a worthy cause in Talgarth. The author apologises for not being able to trace the names of the boys and girls at the time of publication.

CHAPTER 5

Schooldays

147.   Talgarth School 1922. Back row, left to right - B Mitchell, V Brown, L Pepprel, Ms Price, Ms Thomas, H Gladell and D Jones. Third row - M Evans, N Walsh, M Speake, Ms James, H Price, E Price, C Price, E Griffiths, V Brown, Ms James, P Browne, M Jones and M Collett. Second row - E Davies, P Poole, E Collett, Ms Mitchell, P Blackett, G Price, B Fawke, E Davies, B Jones, N Davies, A Griffiths, A Pritchard, R Jenkins, G Morgan, A Levatt, E Powell, L Denis and D Price. Front row - unknown, M Jones, Ms Evans, D James, M Weale, E Price, G Stather, E Lewis, D Davies, S Jones, H Bentley and R Evans.

148. At the school in earlier days and it appears that a traditional celebration of St David's Day is being held. One lady we do know is Mrs E Lewis (nee Davies) who is in the front row, second from the left.

149. This picture was taken at Bronllys School, probably during the late 1950s and includes among others, S Turner, Mary Davies, M Blackwell, S Harrison, Linda Jacob, Billy Millington, R Turner, L Burns, E Hopkins and M Thomas. Rev Phillips is seen in charge at the back.

150. The pupils outside Talgarth School in about 1914 with Maggie Lewis recognisable on the right.

151. Anxious faces at Talgarth School at an annual sports day during the 1970s. Two of the boys positively identified are Ian Turner and Terry Bowen.

152. Talgarth School 1932. Back row, left to right - E Blackett, J Weston, T Gwynne, G Humphries, F Griffiths and T Reardon. Third row - F Collett, J Gwynne, I Conlin, B Powell (Teacher), E Williams, D Thornton, H Holmes, S Williams, I Williams, S Price, B Jones, M Collett and B Mitchell. Second row - G Evans, M Wood, T Weston, E Reardon, D Reed, B Taylor, M Hughes, C Price, G Wilkinson, I Prosser and D Jones. Front row - T Morris, E Lewis, T Lewis, G Prosser, E Poole, C Rogers, D Hopkins, C Parry and D Morgan.

94

153. Talgarth School Standard 4 in 1978-79 and the pupils are pictured with headmaster Mr Davies. Left to right are, back row - Katrina Brooks, Steven Jones, Gareth Lloyd, Tania Bartlet, Ruth Griffiths, Alison Newell and Louise Powell. Middle row - Gethin Davies, Don White, Andrew Skyrme, Michelle Weale, Dena Gwilliam, Sian Turner and Julie Evans. Front row - Kevin Jones, Angela Barrett, Liddy Lewis, Alison John and Delyth Jones.

154. This picture of smiling faces of the youth of Talgarth reveals the following names reading back to front and left to right - Andrew Watkins, David Jones, Robert Stephens, Darren Griffiths, Daniel Cardew, Gareth Lloyd, Malcolm Harper, Shaun Griffiths, Steven Vaughan, Simon Morgan, Rees Roberts, Vernon Weale, Steven Jones, David Morgan and Marco Ditch.

CHAPTER 6

The Sporting Life

155. Talgarth AFC displaying a number of trophies won during the 1971-72 Season. Among the very many players seen here are, back row - V Jones, L Gwynne, W Davies and J Skinner. Middle - L Lewis, R Rosser, D Rose, A Ricketts, K Parry, D Ricketts and J Thomas. Front - M Hughes, A Davies, E Gittoes, T Blackwell, L Wilcox, P Sharman and G Rhodes.

156. The rugby players of Talgarth pictured outside Gwernyfed School during the 1982-83 Season. Appearing on this photograph are, back row - Phil Prentice, Vincent Stephens, Tony Skyrme, Geraint Humphries, Tiffer Hyatt, Ron Smart and Nick Evans. Third row - Brian Skyrme, Kevin Skyrme, David Morgan, Stuart Eckley, Ian Griffiths, Philip Griffiths, Peter Carey, George Williams and David Knapp. Second row - Robert Stephens, Paul Jones, Mark Jones, Mike Smart, Will Rees, Michael Cooper, Chalky Philips and Smudger Smith. Front row - David Toms, Andrew Gwynne, Lyndon Lewis, Jeff Williams, Caerwyn Philips, Ceri Morgan and Brian Jones.

157. The Rugby Club was founded by two former schoolmasters at Gwernyfed, David Knapp and Bernard Altmeyer in the 1960s. Starting with nothing, the players were for many years grateful for the use of a field provided by Mrs Stephens of Great House Farm. Pictured above is the old malthouse which was purchased and completely renovated by voluntary labour to provide a club-house proper in the late 1980s. The success of the club is measured by the fact that it now has a 1st, 2nd and Youth team together with several junior section teams. Chay Billings achieved international status and a number of players who started at Talgarth have since moved on to higher circles.

158. From a bygone age, the Talgarth Juniors of 1925 proudly displaying the year's trophies, the Builth Cup, the Talgarth Cup and the Northcott Cup. Standing are R Morgan, G Jenkins, M Cochrane, T Harper, R Davies, Glyn Davies, T Evans and G Vaughan. Seated - H Vaughan, G Hughes, Alvin Davies and Tom Pugh. Kneeling - E Jones and R G Davies. Tom Pugh was subsequently capped for Wales as an amateur.

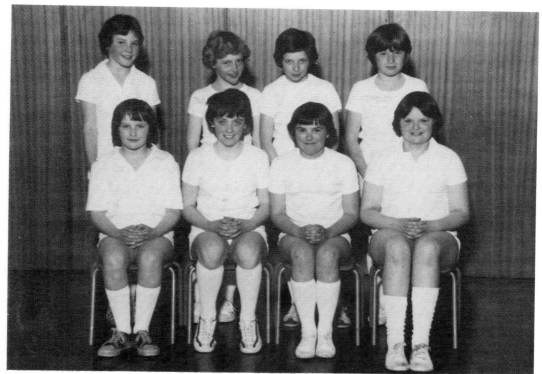

159. Some early learners of the game of netball are these Talgarth ladies of 1978-79 and left to right they are, back row - Michelle Weale, Delyth Jones, Nerys Jones and Sara Parry. Front row - Julie Evans, Alison Newell, Dena Gwilliam and Louise Powell.

The Bowling Green, Talgarth.

160. Talgarth Bowling Green as it looked in the 1930s. A number of changes and improvements have taken place nowadays, in this part of Talgarth particularly the arrival of the houses at Bronant.

161. The 'Under 11' lads of Felinfach Rovers team in about 1977. The faces belong to - P Shepherd, S Graham, J Phillips, M Eckley, P Jones, M Graham, M Lynch, D Jones, R Morris, C Evans, G Lloyd and T James.

162. The Felinfach Juniors AFC unfortunately the names of the players were unavailable at the time of publication.

163. The Mid-Wales Hospital Cricket Team of 1952 and with apologies to the lady assistant whose name has not been traceable, the team consists of, back row - P Reardon, G Humphreys, T Reardon, T Jones, T Hepton and V Moses. Middle row - W Devereux, T Cross, W Thomas, I Davies, D Reardon and B Jones. Front row - D Williamson and B Devereux.

164. The Queen's Silver Jubilee was celebrated in the summer of 1977 and here is an all action photograph taken at Westfields, Talgarth. The sporting event on this occasion is a tug of war and two of the gentlemen taking the strain at the front are Mr David Cooke (former headmaster of Bronllys School) and Dr Ken Harvey (local GP).

165.   Talgarth United Football Team. Winners of the Pendre Cup in 1947. Back row, left to right - B Davies, M Owen, T Fawke and L Moses. Front row - L Davies, S Morgan, W Stephens, M James, T Pugh, D Williamson and M Sharman.

166.   The Castle Hotel team winners of the Municipal Bowls League. In the picture are Mr Jones, J Rosewell (landlord), F Blackwell, R Williams, Gareth James, G Evans and S Weale.

CHAPTER 7

Talgarth Jottings

Some local characters who resided in Talgarth from the early to middle part of this century.

Jack Savigar - This was the name of a recluse who lived at the top of the town, next door to Crescent House. His features were good, his face very white and his long, dark, curly hair reached to his shoulders.

Lizzie the Crate - This name was given to Miss Evans who lived with her brother at the Hendre. Her dress was of early Victorian style with a tight bodice and a very full, long skirt. She parted her curly hair in the middle and always wore a boater hat. She and her brother owned some stock which they kept on the ground opposite the Hendre and in fields down 'Edwards Lane'. Lizzy sold Staffordshire figures, china dogs and other ornaments at a stall in Brecon Market every Friday and Builth each Monday. She travelled by train with her wares in two hampers. When she died in the 1930s, a copper kettle was found to be full of gold sovereigns.

Jossie Thomas - The Lamplighter - He was a familiar figure at dusk, carrying his ladder and lighting the street lamps of Talgarth before electricity arrived in the district in 1911.

Jimmy the Monkey - He was the town-crier, who rang a large bell in the streets and announced important news. He was also the local bill-poster.

Long Hannah - Mrs Hannah Lewis, a tall well built woman who lived in a cottage in Penbont Road. She was one of the last in Talgarth to go 'leasing' or 'gleaning' in the cornfields of local farms and carried the corn home in her apron. It helped to feed her fowls. Her husband died of smallpox and her daughter born a cripple. The daughter was taught to read by her mother and when old enough she was prepared for confirmation by the vicar, Rev D L Davies and confirmed in the cottage by the first Bishop of Swansea and Brecon. Mrs Lewis was a devout churchwoman.

Mrs Norman - The first vendor of Sunday newspapers - Lloyd's Papers. These would arrive by train at 10.00 a.m. from Liverpool via Builth Wells. She also sold herbs such as mint and parsley at a penny a bunch. She lived in a tiny cottage which stood at the entrance to the present-day Queen's Avenue.

Tom the Runner - Tom Davies, the great athlete of whom Talgarth was very proud. He took part in many races and was well known throughout the principality as a champion runner. Tom was also the local carrier.

A Glossary of Dialect Words

Boosey - Pasture reserved for the stock of an out-going tenant until May 1st
Chock - See squat
Clemmed - Destitute, hungry
Coot - A fool
Costrel - A small cask for beer or cider. A firkin
Dout - To put out a light
Earn - A small sum of money given to a hired servant at a hiring fair to make a verbal agreement binding. Usually half a crown (12½p), sometimes a shilling (5p)
Gorby - A half-wit
Hump - To carry
Jag - A small load
Lug - To carry, to cart
Mixen - A dung hill
Moither - To confuse
Nark - To annoy

Nesh - Sensitive to cold
Nub - A small lump of coal. (In some parts of South Wales very small lumps of coal were known as 'rubblings'
Oont - A mole
Perk - A perch (an old linear of 5½ yards or square measure of 30¼ square yards
Pikel - A pitchfork
Plock - A small enclosure, usually triangular
Quist - A wood pigeon
Squat - A block of wood on the end of a pole used by carters to put behind a wheel on a hill so as to rest the horse
Ted - To scatter
Tollat - A hay loft
Tun-Dish - A funnel

Latter-day Skills

Candle Making

There are possibly people still living in the Talgarth district who remember candles being made by hand in farm-house kitchens. The wick for the candles was bought in the form of fine string. This string would be cut into lengths about three feet long; the cut lengths were then hung over a fairly long stick and were hung on it side by side. These cut lengths had their ends twisted together, ten or a dozen wicks being spaced along each stick and up to a dozen sticks prepared in this way.

Meanwhile, in a large shallow container, mutton fat was melted by being boiled in water. The hot fat floated on top of the water and the water collected any solid particles that sank to the bottom of the container which was of such a depth that enough fat floated above the water to allow the candles, or 'dips' as they were called, to be made. When the fat was liquid the wicks, on the stick, would be lowered into it and were then raised and put to drain as the stick holding them rested on two long sticks provided for this purpose. When cool the wicks would again be lowered into the hot fat and quickly raised so as not to melt off the fat already cooled. In this way the candles were slowly built up and after a number of such dips the candles would be of a size suitable for use and when completely cool would be stored. Because of the repeated draining they were thicker at the bottom than they were at the top but no one minded this.

During the process sawdust on the floor collected any fat drippings that had fallen. Most of the family would assist and because it was carried out usually at the beginning of winter it was a congenial task before a warm log fire. The fat was collected and saved each time a sheep was killed for its mutton and because the fat had other uses as well, none of it was wasted. The old folk did not look with favour on 'composition candles' or 'composites' as they were called. They remembered stories that they contained arsenic. This was quite true in some cases for a letter in the 'Glamorgan, Monmouth and Brecon Gazette and Merthyr Guardian,' Saturday, 29th July, 1837 reference was made to arsenic in composition candles.

Soap Making

A feature of life in the last century was the use made of so many things that are not regarded as being of value today. In those days when mutton was the main dinner dish on the farm, mutton fat was used in the making of soap as well as in the making of candles. In addition wood ash was regularly obtained from the bread oven which was, of course, used every week. This wood ash and the mutton fat were used for making bars of soap.

Water was poured on quick-lime and allowed to stand. The clear water was then drained off and poured into a container holding wood ash and mutton fat, and soda. The mixture was boiled and then allowed to cool in shallow dishes before being cut up into the bars which were once so familiar. Sometimes a disinfectant was added; scrubbing soap used for cleaning was almost always so treated, carbolic acid being well known for this purpose. When the liquid had solidified and cooled it was cut up into bars and, in dry weather, put out to cool completely and harden.

In a lecture on 'The Drovers' Professor E G Bowen once reminded a Talgarth audience that when the drovers were setting out on their journey they would rub the insides of the feet of their knee-length stockings with soap before putting them on because of freedom from blisters it gave; blisters being caused by friction between foot and sock were avoided in this simple way.

TRADES (1860-1960)
Saddlers

There were two saddlers in the district during this period. David Williams, whose workshop was on the Path, visited farms during the day to carry out this trade: he was known to most people as 'Doctor North', the reason for this being that he always wore his coat collar turned up!

The other is Mr Roger Vaughan who had his business in Bell Street.

Tailors

There have been several tailors in the district during the last 100 years, but at the present time there is not one tradesman in the district.

Most notable of these men was George Mills of Red House, (Mike Skyrme - Bronllys Road today) Talgarth, who, at one time employed several men to help him carry on the business. He was a first class tradesman and the fact that he always smoked cigars was proof that his business was a prosperous one.

Living on the Bank was another notable tailor, by the name of John Pugh. His business was also a very prosperous one and as well as making new garments, he also did alterations and repairs.

Brewing

The brewing of beer was, at one time, done at every inn in the district and at many of the surrounding farms. Everything was prepared the day before the actual brewing took place. The fire was lit at about 4.00 a.m. on the day, because the 'brew' had to boil for a certain time. The recipe for brewing beer is given below and all beer had to be a certain strength because samples were taken by the Excise Officer for testing. Price of beer per pint was 2½d (1p).

Recipe: Water, Hops, Malt, Brown Sugar and balm.

Maltsters

There were three such places in the area. These were situated at Penbont Road, Trevecca Road and next to Castle Villa.

The duties carried out by the maltster were to prepare the barley by laying it on scrubbed slabs and drying it with large fires. It was then bagged and sold to local publicans for brewing.

Coopers

The trade of 'coopering' was carried out by several men in the district.

Mainly going to the farms, they were made from green wood, which was found on the ground belonging to the farm, all the necessary equipment such as milking pails, casks, castrels and stools. They also made the larger casks for cider making.

One cooper, by the name of Jonathan Davies was drowned in the great flood of 1880, whilst trying to save his donkey which was being swept down the River Enig.

Mills

Three Mills, namely, Cwm Forest, Tredustan and Talgarth were all operated by water wheels, one of which still remains in the centre of Talgarth near the bridge over the Enig.

The trade of milling was run for the benefit of the community and not for outsiders' purposes. The farmers brought their wheat and barley to the miller, who charged one shilling for grinding a bag of wheat and ninepence for a bag of barley.

The ground wheat was used for the making of bread etc, and the barley was used for feeding farm stock or found its way to the local maltsters.

Basket and Besom Making

There were two men who plied this trade; they were William Davies the Green, who was blind and William Barret of High Street. The price charged for clothes baskets was usually two shillings and sixpence (12½p).

Carpenters

The trade of carpenters and joiners has been carried out by many men within the parish, but of all tradesmen, two in particular stand out in the history of the village.

We have Alfred Games, who was a first class tradesman, specialising in furniture making. Although this gentleman did not make much money, he made furniture of the highest order which can still be seen in many of the Talgarth homes today. He had, as his source of wood, the well known Tregunter Country House. Some of the oak out of the house was used in his furniture making and was at least one hundred years old.

Comparative cost of furniture made by him in 1920-1930 was

Bedroom Suite - £20, Fireside Chairs - £5, Plant Tables - £1 10s 0d (£1.50)

The other personality was William Griffiths, who was known throughout Breconshire for his wood carving. In addition to carving the altar and surround at St Gwendoline's Church in 1923, he was chosen to carry out all the wood carving inside the beautiful church of St Mary's in Brecon.

Blacksmiths

Within the parish there were four blacksmiths carrying out their trade. One 'smithy' was sited at the present location of the Post Office. He was Penry Thomas, a well known character in the area who, besides being a very good tradesman, was also a 'wag'. One story pertaining to his activities other than his trade was - when on one occasion he discovered some children sailing in a barrel which he had to repair, he set to and chased them, causing them to jump into the river and get wet. During his smithy career, he changed the site of his smithy-shop to firstly New Road and finally Penbont Road, where at the rear of the shop he had erected a water wheel to pump his bellows.

Cider Making

The art of Cider making has always been carried out in the district by all local publicans. An eventful day in the life of the parish. About fourteen men would assist in the making of cider at each inn and would receive the sum of five shillings (25p) each as well as a good meal and a free drink. The apples were bought by the publican for 1/- (5p) per bushel and the cider sold by him cost 6d (2½p) per gallon.

Wheelwright

There were three tradesmen of this kind in Talgarth; they were Mr John Games, Mr William James and a Mr William Price, of The Green opposite the New Inn.

Stone Mason and Sculptor

There were two of these tradesmen, namely, Mr John Phillips and Mr James Jones. Even to this day, some houses built by James Jones in Talgarth, are in good condition, which is proof of his first class workmanship.

Wedding Celebrations

Much may be gleaned from old newspaper reports regarding bygone customs, and it is from such sources that the following information regarding a local practice which is no longer in vogue.

Weddings have always provided an opportunity for gaiety and festivity, and while, today, this is usually confined to relatives or friends of the happy couple, this was not always so in Talgarth. A marriage in this little town a hundred years or so ago, often meant a day of merriment for most of the inhabitants. This was invariably so if the occasion concerned one of the more important families.

A delightful practice which featured in these nuptial festivities, was the erection of festal arches or bowers, in the streets or other suitable places. These were usually constructed with poles and branches, intertwined with foliage of evergreens and ivy, and decorated with flowers. Banners bearing messages of good wishes for the bride and bridegroom, were an essential part of the display.

It was the trades people who organised the erection of these bowers, and they were arranged so that the bridal carriage would have to pass under them on the way to and from the church.

On the occasion of the wedding of Mr J Peace Jones, chemist and Miss Thomas, Radnor Arms, there is the following report:

'On Tuesday last great preparations were made ... An arch was erected across the road opposite the Radnor Arms. Arches were also erected opposite Mr Willis's (Post Office), Mr Price's (Cross House), Mr Jones's (Chemist), Mr Chamber's (Bridge End Inn), and near the Baptist Chapel; and appropriate mottos were on each of them'.

Hereford Times dated 11th September 1880.

Another report, in 1890, gives a vivid description of the elaborate arrangements made for the homecoming, to Tregunter, of Major (later Colonel) F W A Roche and his bride. Once again, decorated arches were the main feature of the celebrations. Regarding their construction and location, the Brecon County Times supplies extraordinary detail.

'The town had been gaily decorated with flags and numerous arches of evergreen, bearing expressions of 'Welcome' and 'Good Wishes' towards those who had so recently entered into marital bond .....

This delightful custom of the inhabitants of Talgarth, especially the shopkeepers and innkeepers banding together to salute a local bride and groom, continued for many years, till, it is presumed, the modern motor and wider roads, brought the practice to an end.

An Extract from a Newspaper of 1936

STONE AGE REMAINS - Discovery Made Near Talgarth - MAN OF 2000 B.C.

An interesting archaeological discovery has been made by Professor W F Grimes (of the National Museum of Wales, Cardiff), who has carried out recent excavations on behalf of the Brecknock Society, at Ty Isaf, in the Black Mountains, six miles from Talgarth.

After a fortnight's hard spade work, he succeeded in bringing to light two tombs, entirely of stone. One, which has been completely excavated, is about 9 feet long, the spaces between the stones being filled with dry stone walling. This tomb had lost its covering stone, but the other had over it a large slab 6 feet square and weighing nearly 4 tons. The first tomb contained human bones, fragments of pottery, circa 2000 B C, a flint axe, and an arrow-head.

An unusual feature was a large circular enclosure built of dry stone walling, which, contained another tomb. This, however, had been rifled at some unknown period. Commenting on the finds Prof Grimes said - 'The final results of these discoveries cannot be estimated until the finds have been given expert examination, but it is possible to say something about the connection between the Breconshire tombs and those which have been found on the Cotswolds ...the contents are of the same date, and there can be no doubt that the Black Mountains were colonised about 2000 B C by people who were closely connected with the Cotswold dwellers. Indeed, they may actually have come from the Cotswold region themselves.'

On Saturday last, members of the Brecknock Society, accompanied by Col Sir John Lloyd (Hon Secretary) and Prof Grimes, paid a visit to Ty Isaf. In the course of his address, Prof Grimes outlined the traditional conditions of the Ice and Stone Ages in Europe. With the passing of the Ice Age, it became increasingly difficult for people to obtain a living, as there was no longer an abundance of reindeer, wild horses and so on. Then, with agricultural developments in the Near East, a new civilisation spread over Europe, and the period 3000 to 2000 B C was one of intense activity, and a whole series of different movements, one of which evolved those great Neolithic tombs. These were of two main types, the round and the long 'barrow'. In Wales, round chamber tombs were mostly found in the western part, but in the Vale of Glamorgan and Breconshire the long barrows were prevalent.

Passing to a detailed description of the tombs, Prof Grimes asserted that they were closely allied with those found in the Cotswolds; the principal features were the same type, and it was practically certain that the people were of the same stock. His own opinion was that they settled on the Cotswolds first, and then came up the valleys of the Wye and Usk to Breconshire.

Some interesting Facts and Figures from a Directory for Talgarth from the year 1875

Talgarth with the parish of Trevecca 1875

Population figures (1871): Talgarth - 1,408
Post Office: Talgarth - Alfred Willis, Postmaster; letters from all parts arrive at 8.28 a.m. and are despatched at 6.15 p.m. Money Order Office, Savings Bank and Telegraph Office.
Places of Worship and their Ministers: Churches of the Establishments - Talgarth - Rev John Bowen, MA Vicar. Baptist Chapel at Talgarth. Calvinistic Methodist Chapel at Talgarth - Rev Rees Davies. Trevecca - Rev Ebenezer Rees. Wesleyan Methodist Chapel at Talgarth.
Conveyance by Railway - On the Mid-Wales and the Midland Joint Lines. Station Talgarth - William De La Hay, Station Master.
Banks - National Provincial Bank of England. Post Office Savings Bank, Talgarth.
Blacksmiths - Joseph Hughson, Trevecca. David Jenkins, Talgarth. Penry Thomas, Talgarth.
Boot and Shoe Makers - Samuel Griffiths, Talgarth. Thomas James, Talgarth. William Samuel, Talgarth.
Carpenters and Joiners - William James, Talgarth. David Williams, Talgarth.
Chemists and Druggists - John Peace Jones, Talgarth. W M Morris, Talgarth.
Coal and Lime Merchants - Breconshire Coal and Lime Co Ltd, Railway Station. Jones & Co, Talgarth Station. South Wales Mercantile Co Ltd, Railway Station.

Inns and Public Houses - Ashburnham Arms, Talgarth. Bell, Talgarth. Black Lion, Talgarth. Bridgend, Talgarth. Castle Inn, Talgarth. Castle Green, Talgarth. Horse and Jockey (The Limes). Masons' Arms, Talgarth. Plough, Talgarth. Radnor Arms, Talgarth. Swan, Talgarth. Three Cocks (The Hendre). Upper Lion, Talgarth.
Ironmonger - Thomas Powell, Talgarth.
Millers - John Kettle (and Corn Dealer), Talgarth. George Lewis, Talgarth Mill.
Nailmakers - Evan Evans, Talgarth. Henry Morgan, Talgarth.
Painter, Plumber etc - Charles Martin, Talgarth.
Schools - Mrs Margaret Bonnar, Talgarth. British School, Talgarth - Mr Wm Davies, master. Trevecca College (Calvinistic Methodist). Talgarth - Rev Wm Howell theological tutor; Rev J H Jones MA, PhD classical tutor.
Stonemasons - John Phillips (& sculptor), Talgarth.
Surgeon - Thomas E Williams, Talgarth.
Tailors - Thomas Davies, Talgarth. Roger Lewis, Talgarth. George Mills, Talgarth. William Price, Trevecca.
Wheelwrights - John Games, Talgarth. William James, Talgarth. William Price, Talgarth.
Miscellaneous - David James, Watchmaker, Talgarth. E & G Morgan, Wool Staplers, Talgarth. Evan Price, Saddler, Talgarth.

A Century of Events 1850-1950

1851	Trevecca - Establishment of a Grammar School
1862	Trevecca College closed
1864	Hereford, Hay & Brecon railway opened
1864	Market held for the first time
1865	Trevecca College re-opened
1865	Outbreak of smallpox in Talgarth
1866	Cattle Plague - Prayer Meetings in chapels
1867	Trevecca - College Terrace built

1870 to 1876   Annual Camp of 'Volunteers' at Rhosfach Common (except one year)
1872   Foundation stone of Howell Harris Memorial Chapel laid
1872   Parish Church closed owing to dangerous state of the roof
1873   Howell Harris Memorial Chapel opened
1873   Parish Church re-opened after restoration
1875   School Board for Talgarth formed
1877   Market Hall Corner Stone laid
1878   Market Hall opened
1880   New Calvinistic Methodist Chapel opened.
1880   Serious flood in Talgarth (July 17th)
1883   Parish Church new organ dedicated
1886   Ordnance Survey of district
1887   Memorial Clock erected on the Market Hall
1892   Jubilee of Trevecca College
1895   Death of Miss Jane Williams (Ysgafell)
1897   Queen Victoria's Diamond Jubilee Celebrations
1898   Parish Church Tower restored
1900   Roche Memorial Drill Hall opened
1903   Public opening of Brecon and Radnor joint Asylum
1905   Church Bells rehung after 30 years silence
1906   Trevecca Theological College removed to Aberystwyth - Preparatory School opened
1907   Formation of Local Fire Brigade
1908   Church Hall built
1909   Talgarth Agricultural Show founded
1911   Electric lighting introduced to Talgarth
1913   Trevecca College - large scale renovations
1914   Bi-Centenary of Howell Harris' Birth
1914 to 1918   Great War - local men leave for Active Service
1916   Prisoners of War at Tregunter Park
1919   Talgarth Peace Celebrations (July 19th)
1920   Royal Visit of His Majesty King George V, Queen Mary and Princess Mary on the occasion of the opening of King Edward VII Memorial Sanatorium
1921   Town Hall extension opened
1922   Formation of Talgarth Women's Institute
1935   Bi-Centenary of the conversion of Howell Harris
1937   Playing field purchased
1939   Excavation of Ty-Isaf Cairn
1940   Talgarth receives evacuees
1948 to 1950   Trevecca - Renovations costing £10,000 carried out
1950   Public lending library opened

A List of Farms and Holdings in Talgarth Parish in the Year 1860

	Name	Tenant	Acreage			Name	Tenant	Acreage
1.	Tregunter	Evan Powell	342		21.	Garloddau	David Bevan	118
2.	Great House	Samuel & John Prosser	180		22.	Lower Trefecca	Thomas Williams	222
3.	Porthamal	William Bridgwater	418		23.	Trewalkin	David Williams	23
4.	Great Pendre	Evan Powell	13		24.	Penyrwrlodd	Walter Vaughan	137
5.	The Lodge	Sampson Hinckley	44		25.	Heolceven	Thomas Williams	14
6.	Tredustan Hall	Thomas Vaughan	171		26.	Garngastell	William Williams	39
7.	The Drain	Evan Williams	147		27.	Neuaddvach	Ann Watkins	69
8.	Pwllmawr	Evan Williams	10		28.	Chancefield	Evan Bowen	100
9.	Cock	Benjamin David	13		29.	Lower Dinas	David Gwynne	10
10.	Genffordd	Mrs Jenkins	27		30.	Sychnant	J B & W Davies	72
11.	Genffordd	Evan Powell Junior	70		31.	Pwllwrach	David Davies	28
12.	Pendre	Howell Powell	83		32.	Heol Rowland	Benjamin Price	19
13.	Trewalkin	Thomas Price	91		33.	Cwm (70) Penbryn (14)	William Gwillim	84
14.	Genffordd	Evan Powell Junior	138		35.	Wernfawr	John Davies	121
15.	Penllanavel	Thomas Bowen	10		36.	Cwmgynfin	John Davies	16
16.	Llanerch	William Sanders	61		37.	Blaenau Bach	William Edwards	11
17.	Cevenmawr	Joseph Sanders	65		38.	Penyrheol	William Havard	16
18.	Trefecca	Joseph Sanders	10		39.	Rhydybont	Mrs Jones	101
19.	Trefecca Fawr	Walter Vaughan	228		40.	Bailie Bach	John Jones	79
20.	Whitelow	John Williams	101		41.	Blaenau	Thomas Price	46

Name	Tenant	Acreage			
42. Penishar Rhos	Charles Jones	15	61. Pwllywiber	Abram Jones	20
43. Dinas	William James	20	62. Nantygereidyn	Rev David Jones	50
44. Rhos	John Powell	105	63. Upper Tirgwm	John Jones	51
45. Wern	Mrs Prosser	103	64. Blaenau	John Morgan	57
46. Pentwyn	David Gwillim	61	65. Cevennant	Mary Morgan	10
47. Berthfedw	William Prosser	16	66. Dolvawr	William Powell	109
48. Pen Bryn	Roger Ricketts	52	67. Castle Land	Mrs Phillips	28
49. Upper Blaenau	Roger Prosser	37	68. Tir Mary Gwillim	Thomas Pugh	66
50. Troed yr harn	William Watkins	174	69. Gravog (57) Cwm	Thomas Pugh	57
51. Ffos Rhys	Robert Roberts	10	71. Gwerneveth	John Morgan	26
52. Dinas Castle Hill	Samuel Jones	26	72. Tŷ Issa	Edward Parry	81
53. Cwmffrwd (32) Tirhir (18) Blaenffrwd (17)	D Davies	67	73. Pentref	Elizabeth Watkins	32
56. Evel fach	John Davies	146	74. The Old Turnpike		
57. Tirdraw	Mrs Jenkins	34	The rent of the Old Turnpike was £1 14s 10d (£1.74).		
58. Tynffrwd, Pwlldu, Glanyravon	Walter James	50			

The above list has been compiled from the Parish Rate Book for 1860. The spellings are as they appear in that book. In the following notes some suggestions are made about the origin and meaning of some of the names.

1. Tregunter (Tref Gunter)   The home of Gunter. Sir Peter Gunter assisted Bernard de Newmarch.
3. Porthamal (Porth aml)   Many portals, many gates. Porthaml was an important Manor house.
6. Tredustan (Tredwstan)   Tredustan Hall and Tredustan Court, the former being an ancient manor. Tredustan was a non-conformist meeting place in the time of Howell Harris.
7. The Drain (Y Ddraen)   Draenen ddu. Blackthorn. Draenen wen. Hawthorn.
10. Genffordd (Y cefn ffordd)   The back road. The back way.
15. Penllanaval (Pen Llan afal)   Top of the apple enclosure. Above the orchard.
16. Llanerch   A glade, an open space.
17. Cevenmawr (Cefn Mawr)   The big ridge.
18. Trefecca (Tref Rebecca)   The home of Rebecca.
21. Garloddau (Gwerloddau)   Gwerlod is an obsolete word for paddock. Gwerloddau is the plural form.
24. Penyrwrlodd (Pen y gwair clawdd according to T R P in 'Breconshire Border')   Top of the hay field.
25. Heoleeven (Heol cefn)   The back road.
26. Garngastell (Carn y gastell)   The castle cairn. Castell Dinas.
27. Neuaddvach (Neuadd fach)   The little hall.
30. Sychnant (Sych nant)   The dry brook.
31. Pwllwrach (Pwll y wrach)   The witches' pool.
35. Wernfawr (Y Wern fawr)   The big swamp.
36. Cwmgynfin (Cwm y cyn ffin)   The little valley on the former boundary
37. Blaenau bach (Blaen)   Point, end, summit; source. The little summits.
39. Rhydybont (Rhyd y bont)   The ford at the bridge.
42. Penishar Rhos (Pen isaf y rhos)   The lowest end of the moor.
46. Pentwyn   The top of the hill.
47. Berthfedw (Y berth fedw)   The birch bushes.
50. Troed yr harn (Troed yr haearn)   The iron foot.
51. Ffos Rhys   Rhys's ditch.
53. Cwmffrwd   The valley with a stream.
56. Evel fach (Gefail fach)   The little smithy.
57. Tirdraw   Out-lying land.
61. Pwllywiber (Pwll y wiber)   The viper's pool.
66. Dolvawr (Y ddol fawr)   The big meadow.
71. Gwerneveth   Gwernyfed.
72. Tŷ Issa (Tŷ Isaf)   The lowest house.

Many of the above holdings were too small to support a man and they were farmed in spare time, the tenant or owner working elsewhere during the day. Because hours of working were so long this meant much hard work.

From 1870 on, many of them were given up because men were attracted into industry. The holdings thus vacated became parts of larger farms. The whole district seems to have been divided up into small farms and holdings except for the large ones that were former manors. The land was parcelled out to separate occupiers and does not seem to have been included in records that were made at the time enclosures were made. In Bronllys, portions of land were cultivated under the

'Common Field' system up to 1860 when the common fields were enclosed.

In those days the farm buildings were small and to provide shelter for the stock it was the practice to grow hedges to give natural shelter. Many of the curved hedges of the parish were erected for this purpose.

With the coming of the tractor and with the disappearance of many of the small-holdings many of the curved hedges disappeared also, for their shape was a hindrance when ploughing arable land. In addition better methods of housing and more buildings meant that the curved hedges were no longer needed.

In place of these hedges there appeared longer and straighter ones in which great pride was taken, for Breconshire has always been noted for its trim hedges.

Before modern machinery came to the district, the harvesting season was a period of hard toil extending over long hours daily. Wheat was cut with the hook and it was a common sight to see ten to twenty or more men following one another in the act of reaping.

Many of the masons, carpenters, tailors and traders of Talgarth took a pride in their ability to do skilled work in the harvest field. Many of them were also glad of an opportunity to supplement their wages.

Sometimes itinerant workmen would arrive to assist, many of them from Cardiganshire and some of these came to stay.

Barley and oats were mown with the scythe and crops were carried to the homesteads on wagons. 'Gambos' were used on the smaller farms.

The wives and children of the workers were allowed to glean the fields and locally, they were called 'leasers' and the grain they collected enabled them to make a number of loaves.

Threshing was done with a flail and one of these is still preserved at Gwernllwyd. The threshing was done during the winter and a few men would spend most of their winter nights at work, being paid by results.

The grain was cleaned by passing it through sieves in front of a fan roughly constructed. In some cases the work was done in barns in which there were doors in opposite walls and when these were opened on windy days no artificial fan was needed.

After threshing barley an implement called a barley hummeler was used to remove the beard or awn from the barley.

The grain was spread on the floor and the implement thrust down upon it, very much as one would work an earth rammer. The grains of barley tended to skid from beneath the blades but the beard was knocked off.

Sheep

Early writers give the impression that there are few sheep in the Hundred apart from the mountain breeds. This is hardly correct for, although a few lowland farmers occupied holdings adjoining the Black Mountains with a view to acquiring grazing rights, yet there many farmers who did not possess such right, and would need a bigger type of sheep than that adapted for the mountain.

The Ryeland appears to have been the favourite breed for the lowlands, and in the middle of the last century there was a good flock of Ryelends at Tregunter.

The Radnor and Welsh breeds predominated and thousands of these roamed the Black Mountains up to the years 1879 and 1880. These were wet seasons and proved disastrous to flock owners. Many of the farmers lost nearly all the sheep they possessed. The interest in sheep breeding also vanished at the same time, and the quantities of mutton and wool produced annually on the Black Mountains are now almost infinitesimal compared with the years prior to 1880.

The sheep were all washed in natural pools, or pools artificially made out of the mountain streams. Shepherds and all farm workers wended their way to the pools on sheep-washing day. Sheepshearing was an event of great importance in the flock-master's yearly round of toil. Each farm was allotted its own particular day for shearing and if the flock was of any importance, thirty or forty men and boys laboured from early morn to sunset, clipping off and gathering up the snow-white fleeces. Finally, the master's brand was affixed to the sheep ('Piched') and back those hardy little animals went to their mountain haunts for another season.

Talgarth Town Hall and Market Place

In the early 1860s, there was a growing need for a more commodious building to accommodate the ever increasing trade of the Produce Market, now firmly established in the town. The inadequacy of the old Market Place on the banks of the Enig was particularly apparent during the Christmas Markets.

In February 1875, the Market Committee met for the purpose of taking preliminary steps for the formation of a fund towards the erection of a new Market Place in the town of Talgarth. Towards this end an Eisteddfod was to be held in June and a Flower Show and Sports Event in August.

By December 1875, there were definite plans. A yard and stable adjacent to Talgarth Mill was the subject of discussion. A plan of the site was drawn up by Mr J L Lewis, surveyor, of Glasbury and approaches were made to the Earl of Ashburnham, the owner of the ground. By March 1876, a favourable reply had been received and at a meeting a month later, it was revealed that a lease of 99 years at the nominal rent of two shillings and sixpence per annum (12½p), would be granted to trustees, on condition that the building would be used solely as a 'Market Hall or for other public business'. The Trustees nominated were the Reverend J Bowen, Vicar of Talgarth, D J Powell, Bronllys Court, R W Bridgwater, Great Porthamel, G Mills, Great House Farm and J Phillips, Masons Arms. Later the names of Moses Webb, W Games of Brecon and F W A Roche were added.

Tenders for the construction of the building were invited and from the five received, that of J Webb of Hay was unanimously accepted. The sum quoted was £620.

Acknowledgements

The author wishes to thank the undermentioned for their help and loan of some of the photographs included in this book. Sincere apologies are extended to anyone who may have been inadvertently omitted.

Mr T Berry, Mr R J Birch, Mrs Brothers, Mrs M Davies, Mr H Evans, Mrs Hart, Mr G Lewis, Mr A Morris, Mr D Owen, Mrs P Powell, Mr T P Reardon and Mr M B Thomas.

Further books in this series are available from Bookshops or through The Publishers.

Blaenavon Through The Years in Photographs - **Volume 1**
by Malcolm Thomas and John Lewis ISBN 0 9512181 0 7
Blaenavon Through The Years in Photographs - **Volume 2**
by Malcolm Thomas and John Lewis ISBN 0 9512181 3 1
Blaenavon Through The Years in Photographs - **Volume 3**
by Malcolm Thomas and John Lewis ISBN 1 874538 10 7
Old Aberbeeg and Llanhilleth in Photographs - **Volume 1**
by Bill Pritchard ISBN 0 9512181 5 8
Old Aberbeeg and Llanhilleth in Photographs - **Volume 2**
by Bill Pritchard ISBN 1 874538 35 2
Blackwood Yesterday in Photographs - **Book 1**
by Ewart Smith ISBN 0 9512181 6 6
Blackwood Yesterday in Photographs - **Book 2**
by Ewart Smith ISBN 1 874538 65 4
A Look at Old Tredegar in Photographs - **Volume 1**
by Philip Prosser ISBN 0 9512181 4 X
A Portrait of Rhymney - **Volume 1**
by Marion Evans ISBN 1 874538 40 9
A Portrait of Rhymney - **Volume 2**
by Marion Evans ISBN 1 874538 70 0
A Portrait of Rhymney - **Volume 3**
by Marion Evans ISBN 1 874538 41 7
Brynmawr, Beaufort and Blaina in Photographs - **Volume 1**
by Malcolm Thomas ISBN 1 874538 15 8
Brynmawr, Beaufort and Blaina in Photographs - **Volume 2**
by Malcolm Thomas ISBN 1 874538 26 3
Talgarth - Jewel of the Black Mountains - **Volume 1**
by Roger G. Williams ISBN 1 874538 60 3
Trinant in Photographs - **Volume 1**
by Clive Daniels ISBN 1 874538 80 8
Remember Abergavenny - **Volume 1**
by Louis Bannon ISBN 1 874538 75 1
Collieries of the Sirhowy Valley
by Rayner Rosser ISBN 1 874538 01 8
A History of Fochriw in Photographs - **Volume 1**
by Peter Price ISBN 1 874538 11 5
The Flavour of Islwyn Remembered
by Kay Jenkins ISBN 1 874538 06 9
Remember When - Memories of Yesteryear
by Iris Roderick Thomas ISBN 1 874538 20 4
Bargoed and Gilfach in Photographs - **Volume 1**
by Paul James ISBN 1 874538 31 X
History of Webbs Brewery - Aberbeeg
by Ray Morris ISBN 1 874538 46 8
Hills of Fire and Iron
by Peter Morgan Jones ISBN 0 9512181 9 0